Savanna Animals

Written by DEBORAH HODGE
Illustrated by PAT STEPHENS

Kids Can Press

For Helen, who loves adventure of any kind – D.H.

For Caitlin – P.S.

I would like to gratefully acknowledge the expert review of the manuscript and art by Dr. Jake Goheen, Assistant Professor of Zoology, University of British Columbia, Vancouver, BC.

Special thanks to the talented people at Kids Can Press who make these lovely books possible: Sheila Barry, editor; Pat Stephens, illustrator; Katie Gray, designer; and Karen Boersma, publisher.

Text © 2009 Deborah Hodge
Illustrations © 2009 Pat Stephens

Kids Can Press acknowledges the financial support of the Government of Ontario, through the Ontario Media Development Corporation's Ontario Book Initiative; the Ontario Arts Council; the Canada Council for the Arts; and the Government of Canada, through the BPIDP, for our publishing activity.

Published in Canada by
Kids Can Press Ltd.
29 Birch Avenue
Toronto, ON M4V 1E2

Published in the U.S. by
Kids Can Press Ltd.
2250 Military Road
Tonawanda, NY 14150

www.kidscanpress.com

Edited by Sheila Barry
Designed by Kathleen Gray
Printed and bound in Singapore

The hardcover edition of this book is smyth sewn casebound. The paperback edition of this book is limp sewn with a drawn-on cover.

CM 09 0 9 8 7 6 5 4 3 2 1
CM PA 09 0 9 8 7 6 5 4 3 2 1

Library and Archives Canada Cataloguing in Publication

Hodge, Deborah
    Savanna animals / written by Deborah Hodge ;
illustrated by Pat Stephens.

(Who lives here?)
ISBN 978-1-55453-072-4 (bound).
ISBN 978-1-55453-073-1 (pbk.)

1. Savanna animals—Juvenile literature. I. Stephens, Pat, 1950–
II. Title. III. Series: Hodge, Deborah. Who lives here?

QL115.3.H63 2009   j591.74'8   C2008-907068-2

Kids Can Press is a *Corus*™ Entertainment company

Contents

What Is a Savanna?

A savanna is a huge area of grassy land, dotted by trees and bushes. Savannas are found in hot parts of the world. Most have a long dry season and a shorter rainy season.

The savanna is home to many exciting animals. Their bodies and habits are suited for living on the warm, grassy plain.

The savanna is lush and green after it rains. The animals fill up on fresh grass. Munch, munch …

When the rainy season ends, the grass dries up. The animals must travel to find food and water.

Grass is important to all the animals. Some eat the grass, while others eat the grass-eaters.

Elephant

The elephant is the world's biggest land animal. An adult elephant can weigh as much as 13 heavy pianos.

Elephants live in family groups made up of mothers and babies. A group eats and sleeps together. They touch each other often.

An elephant's long, powerful trunk works like a hand to pick grass, leaves and branches to eat.

Bath time! Elephants splash in water or mud to protect their sensitive skin from the hot sun.

Whew! An elephant flaps its enormous ears to cool down. Each ear is about the size of a blanket on your bed.

7

Wildebeest

Wildebeests wander the savanna in huge groups.
The herds cross rivers and plains, searching for grass.

Living in a herd is safer than being alone. The wildebeests use their
eyes and ears to spot the lions, crocodiles and hyenas that hunt them.

If danger comes near, a frightened wildebeest will gallop away on its powerful legs. Hurry!

A mother gives birth in the rainy season when there is lots of food. Just an hour after her baby is born, it can run.

Crash! Crack! Males battle with their sharp horns to win a bigger piece of land.

Giraffe

The giraffe is the tallest animal in the world. Some big males are as tall as two-story buildings.

Giraffes stay near acacia trees that grow on the savanna. A calf drinks its mother's milk, but soon it will eat acacia leaves, too. Delicious!

A giraffe nibbles high in the treetops. It picks leaves with a tongue that is as long as your arm.

Male giraffes wrestle with their powerful necks to see who is the strongest.

Long, strong legs help the giraffe run fast. Hooves, as big as dinner plates, give a fierce kick.

11

Meerkat

The meerkat is the size of a large squirrel. Meerkats live in close family groups that work, play and sleep together.

Meerkats hunt by day and spend their nights in underground homes called burrows. These meerkats are relaxing in the warm sun. Ahh...

Dig, dig, dig. A meerkat uses its long, sharp claws to dig a burrow or look for insects, lizards and other food.

This meerkat is standing guard. It calls out an alarm if a jackal, snake or other enemy comes near.

When their parents go hunting, baby meerkats are cared for by a babysitter.

Zebra

The zebra looks like a horse with stripes. Herds of zebras roam the hot savanna, grazing on grass.

It is safer in a crowd, so zebras often travel with wildebeests and other animals. This thirsty zebra keeps a lookout for lions as it drinks. Slurp!

Big front teeth slice the grass, and strong back teeth grind it. A zebra's teeth never stop growing.

When zebras are together, their stripes seem to blur. An enemy has trouble picking out just one zebra to chase.

A baby zebra is a fast runner. Being able to keep up with the herd helps the foal stay safe.

Black Mamba

The black mamba is the world's fastest snake. Its long, slender body glides along the grassy plain or up a tree.

The snake watches and waits for prey — the small animals it eats. Its color blends in with the branches and helps it hide. Shh ...

The mamba's skin isn't black, but the inside of its mouth is. This snake hisses a warning. Sss!

The snake uses its hollow teeth, called fangs, to hunt rats, squirrels and birds. The fangs give a poisonous bite.

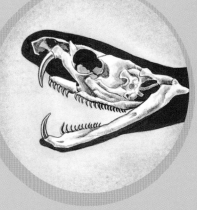

A mother lays her eggs in a burrow or termite mound. As soon as the baby snakes hatch, they are ready to hunt.

Lion

The powerful lion is a fierce hunter that follows the zebras, wildebeests and other animals over the savanna.

Lions live in prides — groups of mothers, cubs and a few males. Wrestling and playing helps the cubs build strong muscles for hunting.

Males, with long, shaggy manes, guard the pride's area. This lion is telling others to stay away. Roar!

Keen eyes and silent steps help this female stalk her prey. Big muscles make her ready to run.

Chomp! A hungry lion attacks with its powerful jaws and razor-sharp teeth.

Ostrich

The ostrich is the biggest bird on Earth. A large male is tall enough to bump his head on the ceiling in a house.

Ostriches travel in groups, looking for fresh grass to eat. Strong legs and thick toes help them run faster than cars on a city street. Zoom!

This sharp claw makes a powerful weapon. An ostrich can kill a lion by kicking it.

Ostrich chicks hatch from huge eggs. One ostrich egg weighs as much as 24 chicken eggs.

This mother spreads her wings like a big umbrella to shade her chicks from the blazing sun.

Rhinoceros

The rhinoceros is almost as big as an elephant. Thick legs and big hooves hold up the rhino's bulky body.

A mother rhinoceros fiercely protects her calf and chases away lions that come near. Rhinos can gallop when they need to.

Rhinos use their horns to protect their babies or fight. Males show off their horns to see who is most powerful.

A long head and wide lips are perfect for grazing on short grass. When this rhino eats, the grass looks mowed!

Splish, splash! A mudbath helps a rhino stay cool and keep its skin from getting sunburned.

Animal Words

Every savanna animal has special body parts that help it get food and stay safe. Can you find pictures of these body parts in the book?

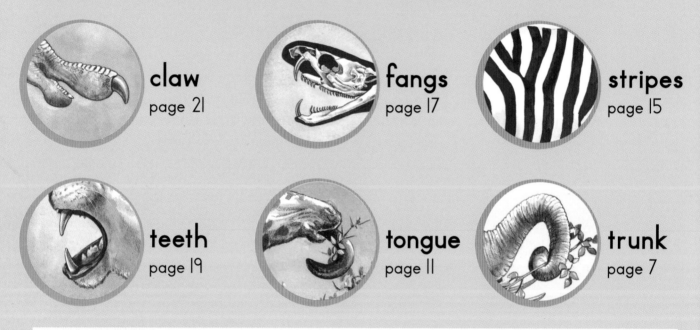

claw
page 21

fangs
page 17

stripes
page 15

teeth
page 19

tongue
page 11

trunk
page 7

For Parents and Teachers

Savannas are found in regions of the world near the equator. They sit between tropical grasslands and forests. Savannas have year-round warm temperatures and a distinct rainy season. The animals that live there are adapted to seasonal conditions that change from very wet to very dry. The open habitat doesn't limit their size, so many animals are big. And, with few trees to hide behind, they are safer in groups. The animals in this book are from the savannas of Africa. Meerkats also live in the desert, and some elephants and rhinoceroses are found in Asia.

Savannas are important ecosystems that are easily damaged by human activities, such as converting them to farmland. If the land is overgrazed, plants are harmed and the savanna becomes barren desert. Sadly, this loss of habitat causes some animals, such as the elephant, to become endangered. Conservationists are working hard to preserve savannas and their species.